Tornado Drill

Tornado Drill

Poems by

Dave Malone

Cover design by Shay Culigan
Author photo by Jenni Wichem
Cover photo by Walter Albertin

ISBN: 978-1-63980-068-1

Kelsay Books
502 South 1040 East, A-119
American Fork, Utah 84003
Kelsaybooks.com

Other Books by Dave Malone

View from the North Ten

O: Love Poems from the Ozarks

You Know the Ones

Acknowledgments

Some of these poems, often in earlier versions, were first published elsewhere. Grateful acknowledgement to the editors of these journals.

Between These Shores Literary and Arts Annual (BTSA): "Ginger" and "Status Update"

Blue Unicorn: "Elegy" (as "Elegy for an Actor") and "Photograph of Two Boys Beside a Barn, 1979"

Catalyst: "High Hopes"

Dime Show Review: "Bolt"

Elder Mountain: A Journal of Ozark Studies: "Confetti" and "Fruit"

The Heartland Review: "Growing Up," "Hairdresser," "Horseshoe," and "To a Coworker I Once Knew in Terre Haute, Indiana"

K'in: "The 9:15 to Memphis"

Midwest Review: "Leaf Blower" and "Rain"

MockingHeart Review: "The Smallest Wren"

Ohio Journal of English Language Arts: "News Story Spreads" (as "News Story in Hometown Paper")

Plainsongs: "Cashier Strays from Register" and "Glory Days" (as Firewood")

Portage Magazine: "Tornado Drill" and "We Bury Our Secret"

Poydras Review: "Summer Afternoon in the Pod" (as "Praise")

Quiet Diamonds: "Fitful Dreams"

Red Dirt Forum: "Leaving the Scene," "Okies Playing Pitch," and "Taking a Walk after Reading a Post on Your Timeline"

Right Hand Pointing: "Heron" and "Recalling Light" (as "Remembering Light")

The River: "Because the Professor Has Been to Contaminated Areas"

River Heron Review: "Pencil a Venn Diagram with an Intersection of Sets"

San Pedro River Review: "King's Ransom" and "One of the Ones"

Spindrift: "Moss Myth" and "Walk in the Woods"

Sunspot Lit: "Promises"

Tipton Poetry Journal: "What Movie Actors Know" (as "I Bet Movie Actors"), "Neighboring Town" (as "Small Town"), and "Middle School Swimming Lessons (as "Swimmin Lessons")

Typishly: "Close Call"

Up North Lit: "Easter Egg Hunt," "Mattress," and "Season's Ice"

Visual Verse: "Portrait" (as "Testament")

Willows Wept Review: "Cigarette"

"Fifi Gets Placed in Timeout" originally appeared online as "Fifi Gets Put into Timeout" at my Tumblr blog and at *Every Day Poems* (*tspoetry.com*).

"Hairdresser" appeared in *Every Day Poems* (*tspoetry.com*) on September 30, 2021.

"Mutt" originally appeared as "Mystery" at the Tweetspeak Poetry website (*tspoetry.com*) as part of a poetry prompt on October 28, 2018, and also in *Every Day Poems* (*tspoetry.com*) on November 23, 2018.

"Weekends at Aunt Gwens" as "Gwen Yang" was posted as an image poem to Facebook and Twitter on February 17, 2017.

"What Movie Actors Know" as "I Bet Movie Actors Know This" also appeared in *Every Day Poems* (*tspoetry.com*) on January 12, 2021.

The following poems also appeared online in the *Friday Poems* series at my website, *davemalone.net,* and in other social media: "Taco Hut Closing Tomorrow" as "Closing Tomorrow" (August 10, 2018), "The Nuisance of Nouns" (September 14, 2018), "Passing Through" (December 7, 2018)

The following poems also appeared online in my e-newsletter, *The Rule of Three:*
"Confetti" (November 3, 2018)
"Fifi Gets Placed in Timeout" as "Fifi Gets Put into Timeout" (July 3, 2018)
"Weekends at Aunt Gwen's" as "Gwen Yang" (August 3, 2019)
"Reading Philip Larkin's Poems at the Lake" (August 3, 2018)
"Crystal Bridges" as "They Hang Art Here" (October 3, 2018)

* * *

I would like to thank Karen Kelsay, Delisa Hargrove, Peter Davies, Shay Culligan, Jenna Sumpter, and Julie Kelsay for believing in and publishing this book. Thanks also to Matthew Brennan and Paulette Guerin Bane who provided editorial suggestions on a good number of the poems included in this volume.

I am extremely grateful to my awe-inspiring, devoted literary patrons. Their support has buoyed my spirit and allowed me quality, creative time. A heartfelt thanks to them: Amy Fischer, Axel Liimatta, Brian Katcher, Clara Applegate, Derek Dowell, Elizabeth Brixey, Emily Edwards-Long, Felix Lloyd, Heather Fisher, Isaac Protiva, J. Kyle Johnson, Jason McCollom, Jessica Nease, Kimberly Allen, Lauren Campbell, Michael Brasier, Nathanael Elbrecht, Neal and Betsy Delmonico, Phillip Wages, Richard Maxson, Sarah Morris, Sharon Buzzard, Steve Wiegenstein, and Wayne Blinne.

I thank my spouse, Jenni, and my stepson, Caiden, for their patience and support. For many months, they put up with my unusual waking hours and wacky schedules that were necessary for the creation of these poems.

Contents

Memory

Quarantine

Finning the Deep

Growing Up

Tornado Drill

Beneath the school desks, our legs angle
and lean like autumn crickets.

Dust motes float and sparkle
above the tongues of our sneakers.

To distract ourselves from the howling windows,
we till the flooring tiles with fingernails

scrubbed clean of bottled glue
and the remains of Mrs. Nelson's

no-bake cookies. She booms, "Quiet,"
and invites the great silence.

We don't wish to hear
what is a low hum at first—

just an evening tractor laboring
several farms over—but then

the earth roars and the sky paints
the classroom windows cocoa.

Some of us scrape wings together and squeak.
Others weep. I scramble to the glass.

Mutt

In the narrow gulley
flat as a shin bone,
we march three astride.
A crisp autumn breeze
crinkles down jackets
as a trio of kids tramps
the dry creek bed at dusk.
Cottonwoods sway and creak;
their ancient heads bob in warning.

Ahead the arroyo rises
like the brim of a worn Stetson,
lined with green prickly pear
and red-berried sumac.
Graves there, everyone says.
Kansa and rancher together
hugging deep beneath prairie grass.

The light grows dim
as we climb. The wind
absent now like a missing tooth.
We carry my dog's body,
shovels. We aren't afraid really.

Fruit

Two old men in a truck
give us a ride to the lake.
Neither of us likes their looks.

In the bed we hunch
amid rotting watermelons
then scramble to freedom
at a four-way stop.

Leering eyes track us
into June shadows
where our slim bodies fit,
fourteen and fruitful.

We eat the lake.
Leave just fish bones and shells.
Our skin darkened into beauty.

When the moonlight yellows the road,
we shiver in the wanting.
Forty miles.

Recalling Light

It is the light I think
I recall. Was it church

or vacation Bible school,
the desks like pews,

when the sun's morning rays
ached to rest on shoulders

while the teacher dimmed
at the front, barely perceptible

like God. I remember now
the gospel the instructor ignored—

how the cypress floor danced
with golden dust in its hair.

Flight

The hardback's spine
shone iridescent blue
like my heaven.

Mother read to me
of Artemis, Triton,
Zeus and Athena,
but I requested most
the tale of Daedalus and Icarus.

The illustrations were inked
in afternoon's azure foam,
a springtime sky I knew well
with its frothy, bearded clouds.

Between air and water
flew a muscled boy and man,
both shirtless and chalk-white.

I was amazed at their vulture wings
and how in summer sun and glory
they floated for a few pages—
until the dripping wax,
until the boy turned upside down.

Middle School Swimming Lessons

Outside the gymnasium, the Ozark
summer sky rippled like worn denim.

Inside, a shrill whistle pierced ear to elbow
then the tinny voice of the teenage instructor

who thought she could teach us how to swim.
There's not much to remember—except

her dunking us into the death of true sound,
like how you get paralyzed during a nightmare

inside the impenetrable boggish fog
then the thud and fade of heartbeat.

Youth Camp

We left our tent to hunt
the early morning light,

a lonesome doe
in the dark woods

approaching without sound—
just the hint of presence,

of blueness,
of breath.

We trekked into the shadows
unsure of our footing

and gained a cemetery of moss,
and with our eyes blind like the dead,

we felt our way to higher ground,
fists groping for the roots of pines—

until the hillside shook
with the stomp of the unknown.

Photograph of Two Boys Beside a Barn, 1979

I catch the pigskin burning
like a roasted autumn beet.
My shadow dances as fire
on prairie grass.

When the camera snaps,
my cousin trails me.
Larger, taller,
he is the one
who should have caught
the deep pass
and scored the six.

Beside the barn,
its windows cast
gray slants of light,
nerve-like cracks
on the yellow field.

The 9:15 to Memphis

The gray man on the corner
gardened most of the year round.

In December ice, he dug up potatoes
more than once. He liked tomatoes

the best, the size of his big hands,
liked them bruised, too, and bequeathed

to us neighborhood kids the meaty black-
and-white-streaked bounty

we used for fastball practice
rather than take home to our folks.

He grew a pair of teenage girls for a while.
Their hips hypnotized water sprinklers in the summer

after they batted wiffle balls into the street.
Their home runs were the few times

they left his lot. Once, I saw the girls
at the hardware store with a wad of bills

buying tomato cages, their eyes fixed
on the bus schedule above the clerk.

News Story Spreads

We know the details.
He was electrocuted
while sitting on a weathered freezer,
one of those industrial-sized jobs,
fixing him into form
as if he were a furry, stiff
bear in a taxidermist shop.

We know the details.
It was Kurt, now as rigid
as any stuffed window display.
Yet we seek those autumn days
to remember him the same:
the surfer hair, the yellow Vans,
the eyes of Lieutenant Cable,
his shadow in the senior hall.

Horseshoe

In the timber behind the farmhouse
a fallen oak yields a narrow path
worn by my grandmother.

A bushy curve hides the bloody sumac
and a future stretch rife
with toe-stubbing limestone—

where a loop turns on itself
though crop dusters swear
the farm's horseshoe good luck.

Okies Playing Pitch

At fifteen I made it to the table.

In my grandparents' kitchen,
golden light shone down

as if God blessed us all, including
Great Uncle Curry and his hand,

full of battle-scarred queens and kings.
During this game of Pitch, my grandfather

served thirst-quenchers in mini-wine glasses
as a good Baptist is wont to do.

Curry dunked his like a genuine baptism
beneath darkened cigarette lips

and asked for another as he worked
his cards over in three fingers,

one he'd left behind in an oil well
in eastern Oklahoma. On his turn,

he nodded to me, his partner,
thick with trumps but scared

to bid five tricks to win the game,
fearful of that hand, of what I might lose.

Weekends at Aunt Gwen's

for Gwen Newberry (1916–1991)

On lonesome Saturdays
Aunt Gwen played a mean organ
when the widowed, western sky
grayed into dust.

On Sunday mornings
she bathed and ran the home
out of hot water—
the Byzantine pipes quiet
in the smallest room.

With ablution complete
and her windows vaulted open,
Gwen donned a white hat,
no matter the dress,
and marched to church.

She *amened* the preaching
until service let out for lunchtime
and tipped at Luby's far more
than a country gal should.

Growing Up

Blue heron babies
small as saplings
flap up from the shore
and crash into cedars
on the bluff.

When my kayak gets too close,
their tiny limbs arch like a bow
my father gave me
when I was a kid
to slay bucks in winter.

That November morning,
I fled the stand for the deep woods,
my boots full of mud and slush—
but then the minty scent of cedar,
so sweet and so young.

Town

Leaf Blower

During my morning meditation, the neighbor
begins her leaf-blowing. She's precise

the way she slides from side to side,
the way she forms right angles

as if acing high school math.
Her noise travels into the hollow

louder than semi-trucks howling
from the bypass. She blows

into blowing into blowing
until a vortex of leaves

half-eaten by mower and storm
form in the narrows.

Here is a full sound. Here is
the *aum* I must have been waiting for.

Confetti

The recycle truck rolls past my office at noon.
I know one of the gals who works at the plant—
a hilltop-thin brunette who banked her dimes
for Loretta Lynn albums when we were kids.

From time to time, I see her at the post office
where she throttles bills under her thumbs.
Or at the mechanic's where her knowledge
trumps his, an off-Jack in Pitch.

She lost a husband to the twister last April.
Sometimes, I wonder about her
as she brooms the recycle room floor—
those scraps of paper, debts and to-do lists,
downed confetti of our town's recent past
she sends away to the paper mill.

Fitful Dreams

A mourning dove lands on the high wires
that float above this town—providing adventure
in phone calls, central heat, and the laundry buzzer
the mother claims her own.

After clothes are folded with Marine precision,
she scrubs the dishes into mirrors
and then wanders into the back yard.
A hammock slices the line between home

and wildness. Near the whispering grass,
tall and tined like a fork,
a robin unearths breakfast,
perhaps spaghetti tonight.
The wind shuffles the frays
in the hammock. She gets in.

She lays her head to the side,
tries to sleep but cannot.
Inside her belly, a poached egg
that claws and unsettles her.

Glory Days

The eldest daughter weed eats the lawn
and lays down the law to her siblings
on how to do things right.

Eager to please, her youngest sister picks up
fallen sweetgum limbs and highway trash—
Pall Mall packs, Bud cans, Sonic cups.

Others mow, trim hedges, upright the bird bath
their stepfather batted down the night before
like fastballs he once conquered in high school,
and as he stumbled into the screen door, he yelled
that Springsteen wrote "Glory Days" in his honor.

The oldest knows this song as deeply
as the sharp blade of the moon when it pitches
down through the forest in November,
when the electricity is gone like the slip
of a ghost, not returning anytime soon.

Status Update

The young neighbors spend a week
in Florida. They plunge their lean bodies

into the Panhandle waters beside gulls
the size of buzzards.

So it begins:

the snapshots she takes, with filters
not praised since Kodachrome dyes.

And they smile, smushed together,
using a selfie stick to frame this lush life,

behind them a barren line of sand and sky.

Portrait

Across the street, the partygoers carry on.
Even from behind the winter windows,

their voices rumble a pitch equal to any train.
All the forecasters predict snow. Snow bricks

and bungalows. Snow bikes riding up the sides
of cars, buildings, trees. Destined after the deluge:

the blowing, like air escaping tires.
Yet, it's the empty flat above the fête

that beats winter's pulse. Through the window,
a single portrait, black and white, left behind

during the last snowstorm, during the final fight
a young couple swore they'd never lose.

Hairdresser

There's something haunting and nihilistic
about your hair-dresser.
  —Robert Lowell to Elizabeth Bishop, 1948

She is twenty and some change.
At times, a spinning top
in a toddler's palm.
Others, the arrow
an ancient archer shot last week.

She wheels us into infinity
in front of mirrors.
At nightfall, she recharges
by traipsing through town.
A coven of bats chirp
when moonlight pours
from her eyes and mouth.

The Smallest Wren

for S.K.

She was small like a wren.
Her eyes too close together.

The August heat is a hammer.
She died in this a week ago.

The evening won't cool
since she left.

Lawns brown and shed
their coats like foxes.

Wrens flee the bushes
and drown the sky in flight.

Pencil a Venn Diagram with an Intersection of
Sets

and you have scratched romantic love
into an oval, a womb, a groin, a belly,

a generative empty, a collective space
of everything and nothing. Here is love

in old age, giant worlds beside it,
circles of memory—how she donned

hoop skirts as a child, raised tadpoles,
painted barn murals of Dante's *Inferno*.

How he nurtured rabbits for 4-H, sweated out
scarlet fever, tongued tuba to State—and all

the geography and personal filmography
of their twenties as they fashioned

their own circles—until they meet
and pencil a widening gyre,

find they don't like to talk much on Sundays
and love the final light of day weaving the woods

in ribbons of color, the smell of upturned earth
on the farm in March, the pluck of the two-lane

that leads into town and how it swoops like a skirt,
how the truck tires rattle and boom like horns.

Neighboring Town

Starlings gloat on the downtown street
and straddle mud puddles.
Gunslingers from spaghetti westerns,
the passerines cock their wings
despite the city ordinance.

They shift their eyes and beaks
to the rafters they've commandeered—
the bank, the drug store, the town café.
One of the city founders, a soft man
in a navy suit, weeps in the shadows.
He feels his fingers still blue
from the final papers' ink.

He recalls the mounds of orange earth
and still hears the bulldozers' clatter
before the strip mall lit up the sky,
before the birds came.

Fifi Gets Placed in Timeout

because she lapsed in judgment
and clawed a mural in the Scando sofa.
The cat's front feet give little fight
when she is placed beside the bath
and made to sit for ten whole minutes—
tough for any feline and more so for her,
a high-minded Calico with plans
of rearranging the living room furniture.

Her adversary, Dawson, a slobbering boxer,
escapes penalty because he ignored
Fifi's amateur artwork. He lies
at the front door on a Pier One rug
where he puts head to paws
as if nothing ever happened
and nothing ever would.

Passing Through

He writes computer programs,
a Christmas card or two,
and a summer check to charity.
Most days, he hides behind his beard.

Wednesday nights, he foregoes church
to host trivia at the local pub.
He tallies the marks on score sheets
of his own design.

He buys a pint for the tax man
who shouts answers at his team
from behind the potted plants
thick as sycamore.

Cashier Strays from Register

After the big tornado, the turn-of-the-century mill
twists itself into a restaurant and tourist machine,
grinding out summer jobs and dollars
for forest families whose ancestors
homesteaded forty-acre patches
of Ozark rock. Muscled semis
deliver new limestone
and cedar to the riverbanks.

A long-time cashier siphons off
her lunch break and churns tired legs
past construction buckets to the river rocks.
Against the stench of stranded bluegills,
a perfume.

She hobbles between crawdad carcasses
and wildflowers taking root beside boulders.
Amid the grass-like nobodies of nature's blooms,
a clump of Downy Phlox, plump and lavender,
thick against her ankles, rich like honey
gleaned from her hives.

Cigarette

The whole world recognizes the beautiful
as the beautiful, yet this is only the ugly.
    —Tao Te Ching

Weeks of effort grant the solitude
of a bite-sized chunk of river,

north and west of most folks
and former timber towns.

In this nook only four-wheel drive
or steady feet know, the water

slows down, gurgles as falling leaves
find passage downstream to another life.

Between two rocks lies the butt
of a cigarette. Half-smoked,

gold and white, like an elbow,
it rests against these aged stones

as if it belongs here
in a holy marriage.

Memory

Close Call

That afternoon in Paris, April hung down
her head and spit. Umbrellas whipped
about like ripped flags. My lover sulked
in our flat with mac and cheese
and graffitied the foggy windows
with her pinkie finger. I'd had enough
of enough and trudged out for a single pint,
a skunky German beer at a tiny bar,
then just left. Left and a couple
rights. It was on a side street
I didn't know. My phone suggested
the shortcut. The rain had stopped.
It was just him and me.

Taking a Walk After Reading a Post on Your Timeline

On your sidewalk
a block from the blues club

the wailing horn,
the strum of bass,

and a singer,
full of scotch and smoke.

She belted out the Holiday lines
as if she wrote them.

I tucked my coat under my chin.

It was a late autumn afternoon,
you know the kind—

when the sun hides behind the buildings,
the air is cold and crisp with wonder,

and you can't be dead.

Leaving the Scene

Journey's "Stone in Love"
brass-knuckled your speakers

and ripped up the street we cruised,
asphalt buckling, and yellow lines

pitching into parking lots,
like bouncers tossing lightweights

like us—but there we were—
you driving 60

down the strip
in the Nova

until we hit the back end
of that guy

on the motorcycle,
and his body pitched up

like a playing card,
and then he fell fast

like an entire house of cards
but louder, louder, louder.

King's Ransom

Should have known
it was all bad news
from the sidewalk.
How the neon red
lit up only the sword
of the suicide king
on that dive bar marquis.
My lover lost at video poker:
a hand, a lunch, a couch,
our stereo, then our rent—
and that's when her fists bit
the wall like the fits
of first love, .
and her lungs boomed
a league of curse words
beside an old man
who shouted
that's not how a lady—
so she dealt him
back to the '50s
until the police came.

Mattress

Like a fish, we carried that queen.
But for two years we'd treated it like a boat.
Dressed up the skiff in white sails.
Uncovered cargo, woke up to sunlight and eggs.
Devoured whiskey and rice, made love
until the moon hummed us to sleep.
But there it was now: this big sloppy fish.
And the rain. We hauled foamy fins and gills
down two flights of stairs where we caught our breath
like the struggling cyprinid we leaned on.
From the stairwell we eyed the green shore
in the parking lot corner. How I wished
we'd looked at each other instead.
It might have changed everything.

Rain

During a March downpour my high school girlfriend and I brush off our homework like the lint from her sweater in the empty YMCA parking lot in that bygone town. It's 3:30 in the afternoon when nothing happens, not even the postwoman trundles down the oak-lined street, and the soccer lot behind us lies gray like cigarette ash, and the inside of my tiny car beams with yellow light like a rural cathedral adorned with stained glass no one can reach to dust, and we've come here for one reason or maybe fifty, and each of them finds a home on our tongues, first there are murmurings about the rain, then there is no language just the blood rush of kissing while snow geese journey northward, and our breath beads all the windows with the lake water from deep inside of us, and we can no longer hear the gaggle in the air, and we are there a long, long time until suddenly we aren't, and we're grown up, and god knows where we are, or who we've become so far from each other.

What Movie Actors Know

I know I drove that Datsun.
I bunked in a shack in the woods.
The Texas sun a red dart most days.
I hitched to Lubbock because the car
failed me for the last time.
The Jemez girl found me at the truck stop.
She was half-way between her life, too.
We slogged to a motel while June rain
sliced the gutters in half. On the balcony,
we held each other for an hour
or maybe ten minutes.
I glimpse this now in the mirror.
But I'm not certain it was me.

One of the Ones

She wears sass like a dress,
all naked knees and shins
bruised beneath a whiskey
she tilts back evenings
at the river shack restaurant,
but it's daytime I'm after,
her honeysuckle sweat,
her side porch groaning
in August heat, her red hair
a torch against the scorched
creek beds that sleep up against
her farm's sides. At night, she hides
in that rocker, all thighs and levers,
love songs and katydid hate,
in a slim wet darkness,
cicada shells and cedar
burnt to a crisp.

Bolt

[bolt] *noun*

A roll of cloth or wallpaper
of specified length.

As in: I sewed through
a humid Ozark summer
with my grandmother,
and we pricked our fingers
over the quilt I swore
I'd hand to my lover
because the fabric
of my ancestors
would bridge the distance
of language that tore us apart—
nine bolts of chambray sky
and plaid river.

We Bury Our Secret

Shovels nick our hipbones
while she and I bury our secret
in her back yard, next to
her children's guppies,
baby teeth, and the gold coins
from last summer's carnival
where she turned away

from her husband
to slay balloons with me
for the bear prize
her smallest daughter
craved nearly as much as
the funnel cakes

we finished
with our fingers
and tongues
in the sugar light
between the tents
until her family
called out for her.

Tinder

Across the café table of steel
and upcycled hardwood,
my date passes her iPhone to me.
Suggests I scroll through pics
of the ocean, punk-rock lyrics,
and tummy-up twins,
her vegan cats,
Sid and Nancy.
I can see the resemblance
between the angry icons and the kittens.

Behind the cup and saucer
of her overpriced coffee,
she hides her chewed-up fingernails
and chuckles at my jokes—
but I can't get past
my desire
for the leftovers
of my salmon wrap
to find their way
into her purse
when she turns away
to ask for our check.

Promises

You made me promises promises
You knew you'd never keep.
    —Naked Eyes

Her red hair thick as bisque
smelled of bourbon and smoke
during our hangover mornings
while the breeze through the corn
snuggled her bedroom window at dawn.
We held each other, ladled in tomato
and cream sheets, burning low.

Once, we pinkie-promised to shave our heads
as the wind picked up and tossed her curtains,
radish and arugula onto the chopping block
of her nightstand. The cold front slipped
into the barber's chair beside her
later that morning. While I kept a silence
in my palm. And curls to my shoulders.

Season's Ice

Recently, I devised a mouse trap to collect
the little ruffians without hurting them.
     —Paul Bushong (1961–1998)

Among his books I found the photo
he'd snapped of the cabin. In golden light,
gas lanterns lounge below rafters,
a necktie from school lurks handsome
on a beam, and the walnut swivel chair
holds a wool blanket for padding—
one of his many gestures to winter
(though mousetraps never made the list).

Perhaps the afghan on the couch
I adore the most—more than
his artist desk with postcards
from that girl in Prague he loved,
more than the papers leaping up
like spring frogs, more than
his paintbrushes leaning to light like trees,
more than the spines of overturned books
camped out and shaped like tents.

For it's that mud-orange and cove-blue throw
and the nights he wrapped it around his shoulders
that warms the memory. And it has to—
because the cabin, the woods, the books,
the free-roaming mice, know the nature
of his gunned-down demise, three weeks
after the snapshot, in the season's ice.

Ginger

You are gone now.
At forty, done.

Your hair, a robin's chest.
Slit-wrist scars, a nest of twigs.
Your freckled legs,
cracked blue eggs.

Behind your green eyes,
distant waves
we can almost make out,
miles and miles
into the man-made lake.

Quarantine

Because the Professor Has Been to Contaminated Areas

In the aorta of the Heartland
a few arteries from the Gateway Arch

he gave a paper inside a four-star hotel
with soft surfaces galore, classically

bent to plush, plush, plush,
and when he journeyed out

of the city's smoky lungs,
he touched down in the midriff

of the Ozarks, and I saw him
in his garage putting up sheetrock

during my morning walk.
The landscape to be a bedroom

for his daughter. He had big plans
and waved me over.

To a Coworker I Once Knew in Terre Haute, Indiana

He's probably dead.
Obituary inked by his sister
and edited more times
than her high school essays.
But there it is.
Commas and end stops.
While she writes,
outside her window
a simple storm quickens
with clouds streaking
like basketball guards.
The rain buffets the panes
with a force like his will
to buff the gym floor
until the maple glows
beneath the high tops
of boys not unlike himself,
hooping, dancing, aiming leather
at the best versions of themselves.

Elegy

for T.C.

The day you died, I mulched trees.
Dogwood, redbud, plum.
What else was there to do?
Planting out of the question
because you fell in August.
Not even a crab apple
would take. And so it is
you leave me, dear friend,
at the tree line. Kneeling
in trimmed grass
where I am to stop
the silent encroachment of weeds.
Sow cypress chips
for natural irrigation.
This was your idea.
All these goddamned trees.

Easter Egg Hunt

A storm bellows in the west.
Like a church alto, it highlights

the lower scale, and she is lost
in its music for a moment.

A mother of one son, soon to be gone,
seventeen and seventy, all at once.

This is his last hunt, the Easter
before his adult birthday,

and she hides the candy
in easy-to-find places in the yard

because of tireless ants,
because of the pandemic.

No pink and purple plastic shells
for his final time, just pure sugar

wrapped up in foil
like a shroud, like a promise.

As the nearing storm wails, she knows
he won't make it home in time.

After the Funeral

No good Catholic at the wake
dared talk about the scenario
we all contemplated—
what really happened
on that early morning
when the ashen roadside barrier
didn't retain his car.

Could the county be blamed
for allowing the smallest of hatchbacks
to hurtle through the iron linebacker with ease?
And did the embankment launch
with forcible contact to the head,
a certain targeting call in this punchy game?
And then there is the unexplained:

his acceleration into the steel defense,
aware of what he'd leave behind—
that job, his family, the travelled canoe.
When metal met metal, he fell
supine and alone in a rock ravine,
deep like an empty, rain-slogged stadium,
yards from any medical tent,
miles from sirens yowling in the distance.

Play Call

for M.B.

During the pandemic,
I watch the highlight reel
from my favorite running back's
first college season
and how he plows
through Trojan defensive backs—
the best part when he guts
the second line of defense
like deboning a trout from back home,
and he's too quick for the safety,
so you can forget the third line—
but that's not today as states lift
restrictions, easing up defense
when they think they've got the lead,
and that's how USC fell
when this immigrant son
was nothing but will.

Chance It

When my quarantine is over,
I want to bet at the horse races.

I want to be that guy at the track,
down on his luck, glad of the rain

as I slide bills under the glass
while mist christens the field

and shimmers on the black manes of thoroughbreds
and the gold jerseys of slight fellows,

and I'll tamp a cigarette then gulp fire from a flask,
alone and cold below the grandstand,

with so much happening in the rain,
with the trotting horses and the cooing jockeys,

with distant clouds crumbling pale and thin like wafers,
like my heart for a girl I knew in school, like communion.

Pentecostal Ladies

Most mornings they amble down my street.
More conversation than exercise.
Their skirts bloom sunflowers,
a decade or two out of favor.
I wave from my front porch
though I know one day they'll sidle up
in their ballet flats and tell me what for.
Like porch-sitting during Sunday services.
Like the nature of those cans in my recycle bin.

But then they'll go direct to their calling:
That Jesus died for me.
That my sins put him up there
on Calvary's cross.
I don't dread their testimony.
I like the way they walk.
So slow. So purposeful.
As if they know something I don't.

At the #10 Station of the Cross

I marvel at the heading, *Gamble*.
Is Jesus gambling on the father
to Zeus the area, including his nails,
and let him limp away to the care
of his pair of Marys? Or is Jesus gambling
on the reward some say he promised
to the wailing thief beside him?

Or is Jesus gambling on us,
that we'll wonder about his years
at Puri Jagannath Temple—
where golden-robed swamis
planted the mustard seed for crops
he wished to sow in the desert
no matter the outcome. No matter
the clothes he'd lose, the dice game
for souvenirs.

We Don't Check Our Phones

In April my spouse and I drive
the blacktop to a hiking trail
where the woods don't wish
to give us a map and grow vines
flouting the best intentions
of the county's caretaker.

We zip sixty miles per hour
away from the virus
toward forgotten homesteads
and paths of yellow flowers.

She and I fight over
the name. Is it jonquil
or daffodil? Which is genus
and which is species?
We do nothing to confirm
or not confirm, and the forest
gives no answer.

High Hopes

He's got high apple pie in the sky hopes . . .
Oops, there goes another rubber tree plant.
　　—J. Van Heusen and S. Cahn

We have high hopes
for how the human race
never ends.

We want the surface of Mars.
We want the moons of Saturn.

All because Mother Earth
sowed within us
the fight-or-flight gene:
Survive at all costs.

But what about the gene seed
that does not distinguish
between *you* and *I?*

Consider the Hawaiian policewoman
on the great ridge of Pali
who saved a boy from jumping,
herself nearly pulled over the edge.

Solar Rays

We won't have to weed on Mars, right?

Unless the hothouse construction crew
dreams of broadleaf or clover or bindweed
or quackgrass or Canada thistle

though the joke may be on the greenhouse gang
since even thistle bears leaves as tasty
as spinach, that will sprawl out like sunbathers
in the Martian dome, eager for solar rays.

Summer Afternoon in the Pod

During quarantine, she buys
a blow-up pool for twenty bucks.

Snags a plastic palm and trashy mags
at the check-out line.

On the hill in the back yard,
she fires citronella candles,

fills the pool with chilled water,
drops magnolia blooms

in its low tide when
her girlfriends arrive,

and she serves apple quarantinis
as sweet as laughter.

Around seven, a storm
tumbles in from the west

like a toddler. But she shoos
it north. To a better home.

Walk in the Woods

At once whatever happened starts receding.
   —Philip Larkin

Last night I walked the woods
lit by the final moon of the month.

Days don't count here
beneath the centuries-old pines

where my grandmother took her solace
on hard farm days, passing up

the washboard or jam-making
for the eternal whooshing

of the forest as much serenity
as yearning.

Finning the Deep

The Nuisance of Nouns

If you dare go
on a spiritual retreat
in the forest,
you may find
it takes most
a couple of days
to venture down to the lake
with fishing gear
and cast out a line.

In the silence
hands often shake
until the bugs come on.
The katydids and cicadas
whir and scratch
while the bass
fin the deep.
If you stay long enough,
there's talk
between you and them.

Voices

after Robert Frost

Amid the deep dark of the forest
the campfire's out. The heat
has withered with the final log
that let go as silver smoke.

Yesterday, perhaps today,
I journeyed alone
into the dimmest shadows
at the cave's mouth
even my ancestors feared.

Despite what must be hours,
the sun makes no attempt to light
the tip-tops of white oak and shortleaf.
And here the only sound's the screech
of an ancient owl before the dawn.

Longtime Schoolteacher

In the hollow rests the house
of the schoolteacher.

The cabin is slim
like a dime novel.

Tattered eaves shine gold
on autumn afternoons.

Saturdays, she challenges the road
with a cane and notebook.

Maybe she scribbles in the shadows.
An abandoned farmhouse sleeps

on a far hill, and I imagine
she gets lost there nights and summers,

sinking into the belly of the house
until divinest feelings come of it.

Sundays, she puts her laundry out to dry.
The clothesline sags from shirts and skirts

spinning in the wind these great circles
like verses she prefers to keep to herself.

Most Just Talk about the Weather

I button up my winter coat
during the season's darkest time.
Inside the truck my breath
casts fog over the windows.
I settle into the chill and drive.
At the hardware store, the clerk
greets me, just two boot steps in,
but I wave her off.

At the counter an exchange is destined.
About the thermals or the work gloves
or the shovel I'll need next month
to spade slim rows for Irish potatoes
in the spirit of desperation or hope.

I unload as the clerk pulls back her hair
and beep-beeps my items. She doesn't think
of last autumn's dead, leaves and mulch
I'll pitch in with withered grass cuttings—
until she lets on about her brother who passed.

Walking Benefit

Sitting at the table with breakfast
I obsess about what I said
the night before and don't taste
the scrambled eggs with dill
and cracks of black pepper.

I go to the sink and crank the water
into white noise and wash the dishes
with more scrubs than needed.

Afterward, I walk beneath the oaks
though I can't hear the crickets' whistle,
instead stay in tune with last night's conversation—
until I trip upon the spreading root of a birch
and lurch forward. Awake!

Tao Master

My schnauzer is interested
in living, which is sleeping,
not in my poems.

A master of schnoozing verse,
he has many forms to choose from.
His favorite, the doggie-ku:

Lie down on left side.
Cross back legs then put nose real
close to carpet. Breathe.

The Widow and the Burial of Peekaboo

No one sees her much.

Sometimes, a shadow
on her front porch.
Then a glowing star.
The scent of menthol.

But yesterday, she staggered
onto my lawn, tiptoeing on gin,
and told my spouse
she took her dog
to the grocery store
and sped-shopped
for the goods
of a widow's week.

When she left the market,
a solar eclipse dimmed
the parking lot.
Through her darkened
Buick windows, the tail
that wouldn't wag,
her Pekingese.

Top heavy with Tanqueray,
she fell into my wife
and plumbed the awful request—
one to which my spouse
did not say no.

Crystal Bridges

My spouse and I return
for the art we've seen before.
I sit beneath the sunrise Rothko.
She finds herself inside the Cindy Sherman.

And the watchful guards flow, flow on.

After a week, an attendant tells us
we have to eat. In the restaurant
teenagers gobble then glide together,
dragon kites above the reflected pond.
We decide to make a winter pact,
joining hands until our wrists freeze
and the sandwiches ice over.

Taco Hut Closing Tomorrow

for C.S.

inked by an aging hand
with nervous cursive
on crooked cardboard
in the yellowed window.
You were ten and very old.
You leaned over the taco meat,
shredded cheddar, iceberg lettuce.
Your nose puckered into a heart.
You cried, dried tears, then ate.

Reading Philip Larkin's Poems at the Lake

At a tidy rental on the lake,
there is no better read than Larkin.
The begonias bookend the dock.
The mid-mod chairs shine like baldness.
The fox's fur slicks back like a stone.
Even the cicadas lash out in rhythm.
Here, there is little wanting.
Except perhaps the roar of a jet plane
or the wail of children.

Moss Myth

Nature always wins.
  —Patrick Beausoleil, 1992

The moss overtakes the back yard.
She whispers, "Oh yes, I dare, I dare,"

as she pirates more muddy land.
On a late spring day I tramp down

the hill to spy her bathing,
her spongy midriff adrift in dew.

She invites me to take part,
to discover the very middles

of both of us, our verdant roaring tufts,
our mutual expanse in morning fog,

so I agree to agree and she consumes me,
her, us, the rain, and in a sweep of shoots,

the blind oak, the upper yard,
the lower deck, and finally that wooden

structure I once called home.

Turn

The autumn trees turn
like friends you once
counted on.

Crisp knuckles—
gold, orange, red—
pound city street
and forest, too.

In the background, aubergine,
maybe beet-drenched, maples
don't say much. But stick
until late November.

Magnolia

Those poor magnolia leaves.
How they hang on.

In the slightest autumn breeze,
how delicate their dance,

this rocking back and forth,
clinging to the central hub of the branch,

their mottled brown stems,
thin legs broken and healed up again

      but wait—

suddenly the wind gusts.
And some they drop.

Surprise!

Heron

I startled the great blue heron
when my kayak scratched stones
in the river's low summer water.
With little effort, like the way
one takes off shoes, the grand bird
flapped long arms, held steady,
until she found the shore opposite me
and slipped into the sycamores
below the bluff. She stayed there
a long time, longer than my life.

About the Author

Dave Malone is a poet and writer. He holds an MA from Indiana State and a BA from Ottawa University. His poems have appeared in *Elder Mountain, Plainsongs,* and *Midwest Review,* and one of his poems was featured on Michel Martin's NPR program *Tell Me More.* He lives in the Missouri Ozarks and can be found online at *davemalone.net.*